The Ultimate Iced Coffee Cookbook

How to Make Amazing Iced Coffee at Your Home

BY: Alicia T. White

License Note!

I know you've read this and seen this in many other books and movies. Still, there's a reason why authors and filmmakers are so adamant about protecting their copyrights despite it being so annoying for you to see yet again… The thing is, lots of people infringe on copyrights, and this greatly affects our work negatively.

Thus, here we go again just so things are clear:

Do not make any print or electronic reproductions, sell, re-publish, or distribute this book in parts or as a whole unless you have express written consent from me or my team.

I spent over 4 months working on this cookbook, so I protect it like it's my baby! I know you can understand the value of working hard on something and wanting to protect your end product, so please help me by not infringing on the copyright or letting others do so.

Thanks!

Table of Contents

Introduction:

If you're like a lot of people then you NEED coffee every day, because you just don't feel like the same person when you don't have caffeine. But, if you're like a lot of people you don't want to drink hot bitter coffee drinks, well that's where this book comes in you'll learn how to make everything from cold brew to flavored iced coffees.

So if you're ready to start learning how to make iced coffee drinks like a barista then turn the page and start making iced coffee now!

OOOOOOOOOOOOOOOOOOOOOOOOOOOOOOOOOOOO

1. Coffee, Oat & Banana Smoothie

Serving Sizes: 1

Duration: 10 minutes

Ingredient List:

- 2 shots of fresh espresso
- 2 tbsp. oats
- 1 banana
- 1 tbsp. honey
- Cinnamon to sprinkle

OOOOOOOOOOOOOOOOOOOOOOOOOOOOOOOOOOOOOOOO

How to Cook:

A. Pour the espresso into a blender along with a cup of ice.
B. Peel the banana and add it straight to the blender.
C. Add the oats and honey, then blend until smooth.
D. Sprinkle a little cinnamon on top and enjoy!

2. Orange & Cardamom Cold-Brew Coffee

Serving Sizes: 4

Duration: 10 minutes + 12 hours refrigeration

Ingredient List:

- 12 cardamom pods
- 7 oz. fresh ground coffee
- 4 tsp. sugar
- 2 tsp. orange extract
- 1 cup soya milk

OOOOOOOOOOOOOOOOOOOOOOOOOOOOOOOOOOOOOOOO

How to Cook:

A. Place the coffee, sugar, and cardamom pods in a large jug or container.

B. Pour on 4 cups of water and refrigerate for 12 hours.

C. After refrigeration, strain the coffee to remove the grounds and cardamom pods.

D. Mix the soya milk and orange extract together.

E. Pour the coffee into glasses so that they're 2/3 of the way full. Then, add a few ice cubes, and ¼ of a cup of the soya milk and orange extract mixture into each glass. Enjoy!

3. Salted Caramel Iced Coffee

Serving Sizes: 4

Duration: 20 minutes

Ingredient List:

- 17 fl oz. fresh coffee
- 8 fl oz. almond milk
- 4 ¼ fl oz. double cream
- 3 ½ oz. butter
- 2 ¼ oz. muscovado sugar
- 2 ¼ oz. caster sugar
- 2 tbsp. golden syrup
- 1 tsp. vanilla extract
- A pinch of salt
- Whipped cream to top
- Caramel sprinkles or something else for topping

OOOOOOOOOOOOOOOOOOOOOOOOOOOOOOOOOOOOOO

How to Cook:

A. First, we need to make the salted caramel sauce. In a saucepan, add the butter, muscovado sugar, and caster sugar. Let the mixture melt over a low heat, but resist the urge to stir. Once the mixture begins to simmer, mix it by swirling the pan. Leave it to simmer for 4 minutes. Then, stir in the vanilla extract and double cream. Add the salt, to taste. Let the mixture simmer for 2 minutes or so until you see it beginning to thicken. Remove from the heat once the sauce is thick.

B. Into a blender, add about 6 cups of ice cubes, along with the coffee, almond milk, vanilla extract, and 4 tbsp. of the salted caramel sauce. Blend until smooth.

C. Drizzle more of the caramel sauce around the inside of the jar or glass, and then divide the mixture evenly between the glasses.

D. Top with whipped cream, more salted caramel sauce, and sprinkles.

4. Coconut Iced Coffee

Serving Sizes: 1

Duration: 15 minutes

Ingredient List:

- 2 tbsp. desiccated coconut
- 1 cup of fresh coffee
- 1 tbsp. coconut sugar
- 1/3 cup whipped coconut cream
- ¼ cup coconut milk

OOOOOOOOOOOOOOOOOOOOOOOOOOOOOOOOOOOOO

How to Cook:

A. Preheat the oven to 350 °F and line a baking tray with parchment paper.
B. Spread the coconut out on the baking tray and pop it into the oven. Toast for 5-10 minutes until the coconut is nicely toasted, but obviously not burned.
C. Stir the coconut sugar into the coffee to dissolve.
D. Fill a tall glass with ice cubes.
E. Pour the coffee into the glass, and then the coconut milk.
F. Top with the whipped cream and toasted coconut and enjoy!

5. Ice Cream Sundae Coffee

Serving Sizes: 2

Duration: 10 minutes

Ingredient List:

- 4 scoops vanilla ice cream (or another ice cream of your choice)
- 2 cups fresh coffee
- 1 cup whipping cream
- 1 tbsp. icing sugar
- Chocolate sauce
- Toppings of your choice! What would you put on a sundae? Wafers, nuts, chocolate sprinkles, butterscotch sauce, fudge pieces? The sky is the limit!

OOOOOOOOOOOOOOOOOOOOOOOOOOOOOOOOOOOOO

How to Cook:

A. Whisk the cream into stiff peaks.
B. Drizzle chocolate sauce around the inside of the glasses.
C. Add a scoop of ice cream to the bottom of each glass.
D. Then, pour half a cup of coffee over the top.
E. Add another scoop of ice cream and the rest of the coffee.
F. Top with the whipped cream and the toppings of your choice and enjoy!

6. Granita di Caffee

Serving Sizes: 6

Duration: 15 minutes + 4 hours freezing time

Ingredient List:

- 3 cups fresh coffee
- 2 tbsp. coffee liqueur
- 1 tsp. vanilla extract
- ¾ cup sugar
- ¾ cup whipped cream

OOOOOOOOOOOOOOOOOOOOOOOOOOOOOOOOOOOOOO

How to Cook:

A. Mix the sugar, vanilla extract, and coffee liqueur into the hot coffee. Stir until everything is dissolved.

B. Pour the mixture onto a baking tray.

C. Freeze the mixture for an hour.

D. Once you see it starting to become slushy around the edges, rake through the mixture using a fork to break the big ice crystals up.

E. Repeat the 'raking' every 30 minutes, until the mixture is completely frozen and broken down into little grains.

F. Whip the cream into stiff peaks.

G. Scoop the granita into the Martini glass, add a dollop of whipped cream and enjoy!

7. Date Caramel Coffee Smoothie

Serving Sizes: 1

Duration: 5 minutes + overnight freezing

Ingredient List:

- 4 pitted dates
- 1 frozen banana
- ½ cup fresh coffee
- ½ cup soya milk
- ¼ tsp. vanilla extract

OOOOOOOOOOOOOOOOOOOOOOOOOOOOOOOOOOOOOO

How to Cook:

A. The night beforehand, freeze the banana. You can either freeze it whole or peel and chop it first - the choice is yours, possibly depending on how well you think your blender will be able to cope with a full frozen banana in the morning!

B. The next day, add the frozen banana into a blender, along with the dates, coffee, soya milk, and vanilla extract.

C. Blitz everything up until smooth and enjoy!

8. Pecan Cinnamon Roll Coffee Smoothie

Serving Sizes: 1

Duration: 10 minutes + overnight freezing

Ingredient List:

- 2 tbsp. raisins
- 2 tbsp. pecans
- 1 banana
- 1 tsp. ground cinnamon
- 2/3 cup almond milk
- ½ cup plain low-fat yogurt
- ½ cup fresh coffee
- ½ tsp. vanilla extract

OOOOOOOOOOOOOOOOOOOOOOOOOOOOOOOOOOOO

How to Cook:

A. The night beforehand, freeze the banana. Also, pour your fresh coffee into an ice cube tray and freeze it overnight to make coffee ice cubes.
B. The next day, in a blender, add the raisins, pecans, cinnamon, almond milk, and vanilla extract.
C. Then, add the yogurt, frozen banana (please peel it first!), and coffee ice cubes.
D. Pour into a glass, and top with a little extra cinnamon. Then, enjoy!

9. Ca Phe Da (Vietnamese Coffee)

Serving Sizes: 1

Duration: 5 minutes

Ingredient List:

- 3 tbsp. sweetened condensed milk
- 1 cup fresh espresso

OOOOOOOOOOOOOOOOOOOOOOOOOOOOOOOOOOOOOOO

How to Cook:

A. Spoon the sweetened condensed milk into the bottom of the glass.

B. Pour the fresh coffee over the top and stir.

C. Add in your desired amount of ice cubes and stir well to chill the whole coffee before serving.

D. Tips: I'm sure I don't need to tell you this but remember that the more ice cubes you have, the more watered down your drink will get when they melt!

E. As an alternative, you can scoop the condensed milk on top, and leave it to sink down. This looks a little cooler, I think.

10. Reese's Coffee Milkshake

Serving Sizes: 2

Duration: 25 minutes

Ingredient List:

- 4 Reese's peanut butter cups
- 2 cups chocolate ice cream
- 2 tbsp. Reese's peanut butter chocolate spread (or, 1 tbsp. smooth peanut butter and 1 tbsp. chocolate spread)
- 1 ½ cups fresh coffee
- Whipped cream to top

OOOOOOOOOOOOOOOOOOOOOOOOOOOOOOOOOOOO

How to Cook:

A. Blend together the ice cream, Reese's spread (or the alternatives) and coffee, until smooth.
B. Pour evenly between 2 glasses.
C. Roughly chop 2 of the peanut butter cups.
D. Out of the other 2 cups, cut a small triangle so that the cup can sit on the rim of the glass.
E. Top the milkshake with the chopped Reese's and set the other cup on the rim of the glass. Enjoy!

11. Nutty Mocha Smoothie

Serving Sizes: 2

Duration: 5 minutes

Ingredient List:

- 2 tbsp. cocoa powder
- 2 tbsp. chia seeds
- 1 cup fresh coffee
- 1 cup coconut milk
- 1 tbsp. almond butter
- ¼ cup almonds
- ¼ cup cashews

OOOOOOOOOOOOOOOOOOOOOOOOOOOOOOOOOOOO

How to Cook:

A. Into a blender, put the cocoa powder, chia seeds, coffee, coconut milk, almond butter, almonds, and cashews.
B. Add 1 heaped cup of ice.
C. Blend until smooth. Then, divide between 2 glasses and enjoy!

12. Iced Cappuccino

Serving Sizes: 1

Duration: 5 minutes

Ingredient List:

- 1 cup fresh coffee
- 1 cup skimmed milk
- 1 tsp. sugar (optional)
- Cinnamon or chocolate to sprinkle

OOOOOOOOOOOOOOOOOOOOOOOOOOOOOOOOOOOOOO

How to Cook:

A. If you take sugar in your coffee, stir the sugar through the coffee to dissolve.

B. Then, mix together the coffee and half of the milk.

C. Fill a glass halfway full with ice and pour the coffee in.

D. Pour the remaining milk into a jar and screw the lid on tightly. Then, shake with all your might to fill the jar almost to the top with foamy bubbles.

E. Remove the lid of the jar, and microwave, uncovered, for 30 seconds.

F. Then, spoon however much foam you desire onto the top of your coffee, and sprinkle with your choice of cinnamon or chocolate, or both!

13. Iced Pumpkin Spice Coffee

Serving Sizes: 4

Duration: 10 minutes

Ingredient List:

- 6 tsp. espresso powder
- 2 cups almond milk
- 1 1/3 cups sweetened condensed milk
- 1 ¼ cups pumpkin purée
- ¾ tsp. pumpkin pie spice
- ¼ tsp. cinnamon

OOOOOOOOOOOOOOOOOOOOOOOOOOOOOOOOOOOOO

How to Cook:

A. Blend the pumpkin with 2 cups of ice and 1 cup of almond milk.
B. Stir together the espresso powder, condensed milk, pumpkin pie spice, remaining almond milk, and cinnamon. Taste and adjust the spice level to your liking.
C. Place the spice mixture in the blender and blend until everything is smooth.
D. Pour into a glass, sprinkle a little extra cinnamon on top, and enjoy!

14. Dublin Iced Coffee

Serving Sizes: 2

Duration: 10 minutes

Ingredient List:

- 4 fl oz. fresh coffee
- 4 fl oz. Guinness (or another stout, but come on, make the effort!)
- 3 fl oz. Irish whiskey (Jameson's being my personal favorite)
- 2 tsp. brown sugar
- 1 fl oz. double cream
- Cinnamon to sprinkle

OOOOOOOOOOOOOOOOOOOOOOOOOOOOOOOOOOOOO

How to Cook:

A. Whilst the coffee is hot, stir the brown sugar into it to dissolve.

B. Fill the glasses about halfway up with ice.

C. Mix together the coffee, Guinness, and whiskey, then divide it between your glasses. Stir well to ice the mixture.

D. Slowly and gently pour half of the cream into each glass from above. This will get you that effect of the cream slowly moving down and mixing with the coffee and it just looks really great.

E. Sprinkle a little cinnamon powder on top and enjoy!

15. Snickers Iced Coffee

Serving Sizes: 1

Duration: 15 minutes

Ingredient List:

- 3 tbsp. caramel sauce
- 2 tbsp. dark chocolate chips
- 1 ¼ cups fresh coffee
- ½ cup almond milk

OOOOOOOOOOOOOOOOOOOOOOOOOOOOOOOOOOOOOO

How to Cook:

A. In a pan, heat the almond milk with the chocolate chips and caramel sauce.

B. Then, remove from the heat and stir in the coffee.

C. Fill a tall glass 1/3 of the way up with ice, and pour the coffee on top.

D. Mix well to ice the drink and enjoy!

16. Oreo Coffee Milkshake

Serving Sizes: 2

Duration: 10 minutes

Ingredient List:

- 10 Oreos
- 4 scoops vanilla ice cream
- 2 cups milk
- 2 tbsp. sugar
- 2 tsp. instant espresso powder
- Chocolate sauce to garnish

OOOOOOOOOOOOOOOOOOOOOOOOOOOOOOOOOOOOO

How to Cook:

A. First, process 3 of the Oreos down into a powder and set aside.

B. Take your serving glasses, and spread the chocolate sauce around the rim. Then, roll the rim of the glass into the powdered Oreos to create a ring.

C. Then, drizzle some more chocolate sauce around the inside of the glass.

D. Blend together the milk, espresso powder, and sugar.

E. Then, add in 2 scoops of vanilla ice cream and 6 of the Oreos and blend. Taste and add more sugar if necessary (but I'm sure it won't be!), or, of course, coffee!

F. Divide the mixture evenly between the 2 glasses leaving at least a 2-inch gap between the milkshake and the top of the glass.

G. Add another scoop of vanilla ice cream on top of each glass, and garnish with half an Oreo. Sprinkle on any remaining Oreo powder and there you have it!

17. Peppermint & Coconut Frappe

Serving Sizes: 2

Duration: 5 minutes

Ingredient List:

- 1 cup fresh coffee
- 1 cup coconut milk
- 1 tbsp. cacao nibs (optional)
- 1 tbsp. coconut oil
- 1 tsp. sugar
- ½ tsp. peppermint extract
- Fresh mint leaves to garnish

OOOOOOOOOOOOOOOOOOOOOOOOOOOOOOOOOOOOO

How to Cook:

A. Into a blender, add the coffee, coconut milk, coconut oil, sugar, and peppermint extract. Also add the cacao nibs, if you are using them.
B. Then, add a cup of ice and blend. Begin on a low setting, and once you see it coming together, increase the speed to get a delightful frothiness.
C. Test the flavor and add more sugar or peppermint if required.
D. Pour the frappe into 2 tall glasses, and garnish with fresh mint and extra cacao nibs.

18. Blackforest Frappe

Serving Sizes: 1

Duration: 5 minutes + overnight refrigeration

Ingredient List:

- 2 tbsp. sugar
- 2 tbsp. cherry juice
- 1 ½ cups fresh coffee
- 1 tbsp. cocoa powder
- ½ cup coconut milk
- ½ cup cherries
- Whipped cream for topping
- Maraschino cherry for topping

OOOOOOOOOOOOOOOOOOOOOOOOOOOOOOOOOOOO

A. **How to Cook:**
B. The night before, pour the coffee into the ice cubes tray and freeze it to make coffee ice cubes. Also, pop your cherries in to freeze.
C. The next day, add the coffee ice cubes into a blender, along with the frozen cherries, cherry juice, sugar, coconut milk, and cocoa powder. Blend until smooth.
D. Pour into a tall glass, and top with the cream.
E. Pop your cherry on top and enjoy!

19. Frozen Tiramisu Coffee

Serving Sizes: 2

Duration: 10 minutes

Ingredient List:

- 6 ladyfinger cookies
- 2 tbsp. Tia Maria
- 2 tbsp. sugar
- 2 tbsp. chocolate sauce + extra for drizzling
- 2 tbsp. mascarpone cheese
- ¾ cup fresh coffee
- ½ cup almond milk
- ½ tsp. almond extract
- Whipped cream for topping
- Chocolate shavings or sprinkles for topping

OOOOOOOOOOOOOOOOOOOOOOOOOOOOOOOOOOOO

How to Cook:

A. Into a blender, add the coffee, chocolate syrup, mascarpone cheese, sugar, almond extract, Tia Maria, and 4 of the ladyfingers.
B. Then, add in 2 cups of ice and blend until smooth. Don't forget to taste and adjust the sweetness, or almond flavor, (or the alcohol level!) if necessary.
C. Drizzle the inside of your glasses with additional chocolate sauce, and then pour the coffee evenly between the 2 glasses.
D. Top with whipped cream and chocolate shavings. Pop an extra ladyfinger into the whipped cream and enjoy!

20. Boozy Mocha Funshake

Serving Sizes: 2

Duration: 10 minutes

Ingredient List:

- 3 cups coffee ice cream
- 2 cups vanilla ice cream
- 2 cups chocolate cereal + extra for topping
- 2 fl oz. Bailey's Irish cream
- 2 fl oz. Kahlua
- 2 shots espresso
- 2 tbsp. chocolate sauce + extra for topping
- Whipped cream for topping
- Chocolate sprinkles for topping
- Mini marshmallows for topping
- Caramel popcorn for topping

OOOOOOOOOOOOOOOOOOOOOOOOOOOOOOOOOOOO

How to Cook:

A. Into a blender, add the chocolate cereal, coffee ice cream, vanilla ice cream, espresso, Bailey's Irish Cream, Kahlua, and chocolate sauce.

B. Blitz until everything is blended, adding a splash of milk to help the mixture if needed.

C. Drizzle some chocolate sauce along the inside of the serving glass.

D. Divide the milkshake between the glasses and top with a generous squirting of whipped cream.

E. Drizzle on the extra chocolate sauce, and then decorate with chocolate sprinkles, mini marshmallows, caramel popcorn, and chocolate cereal and enjoy!

21. Superfood Coffee Smoothie

Serving Sizes: 1

Duration: 45 minutes

Ingredient List:

- 1 cup fresh coffee
- 1 cup almond milk
- 1 tbsp. cacao nibs
- 1 tsp. maca powder
- 1 tsp. coconut oil
- 1 tsp. honey
- ½ tsp. turmeric
- ½ tsp. vanilla extract
- Pinch of cayenne pepper
- Cinnamon to sprinkle

OOOOOOOOOOOOOOOOOOOOOOOOOOOOOOOOOOOO

How to Cook:

A. First, blend together the cacao nibs, almond milk, and coffee.
B. Now, begin adding the other ingredients. I would suggest adding only half of the specified amount of each first. Then, you can taste and adjust the balance to your liking.

22. Iced Dirty Chai

Serving Sizes: 2

Duration: 15 minutes

Ingredient List:

- 2 black tea bags
- 2 shots of espresso
- 2 cloves
- 1-star anise
- 1 tsp. brown sugar
- ½ cup soya milk
- ¼ tsp. cardamom
- ¼ tsp. cinnamon
- Pinch of nutmeg
- Pinch of ginger

OOOOOOOOOOOOOOOOOOOOOOOOOOOOOOOOOOOOO

How to Cook:

A. Pour 2 cups of water into a saucepan and begin bringing it up to a simmer.

B. When you see the first bubbles starting to appear, toss in the tea bags, star anise, cloves, cardamom, cinnamon, nutmeg, and ginger. Bring it to a boil and then allow it to simmer for 5 minutes.

C. Meanwhile, dissolve the sugar by stirring it into your espresso.

D. Strain your chai mixture, discarding the tea bags and spices.

E. Fill a large glass just less than halfway full with ice, and then add in a shot of espresso.

F. Add 1 cup of the chai into the glass, and top up with milk.

23. The Frozen Caramel Macchiato of Your Dreams

Serving Sizes: 4

Duration: 60 minutes + overnight refrigeration

Ingredient List:

- 8 ¾ oz. brown sugar
- 8 mini pretzels
- 8 coffee beans
- 4 cups fresh coffee
- 3 ½ oz. butter
- 3 ½ fl oz. sweetened condensed milk
- 2 ½ cups milk
- 1 ¾ oz. white chocolate
- 1 tsp. golden syrup
- ¼ cup caramel syrup
- ¼ cup dark chocolate
- Whipped cream for topping
- Pinch of salt
- Caramel sprinkles for topping

ooooooooooooooooooooooooooooooooooo

How to Cook:

A. The night beforehand, let's make all of our components so that we're ready for assembly the next day. Stir the caramel syrup into the fresh coffee. Pour it into ice cube trays and freeze.

B. Let's also make our caramel sauce ahead of time, to give it an extra chance to thicken overnight. Put a saucepan over low-medium heat, and add in 7 oz. of brown sugar, ½ a cup of milk, and 2 oz. of butter. Allow the sugar to dissolve. Begin to whisk while the sauce thickens, for 5-7 minutes. Add salt to taste and leave to thicken for another minute. Pour into a jar and refrigerate overnight.

C. Place the pretzels on a baking tray lined with parchment paper. Dip each one into the caramel sauce and pop it back onto the tray. Melt the dark chocolate and then drizzle it over the pretzels off of the back of a spoon. Refrigerate to harden.

D. Also dip the coffee beans into the dark chocolate and then leave them on the tray with the pretzels to harden.

E. The last element to make is the caramel fudge. Line a baking tray with parchment paper. Chop the white chocolate into small pieces. Into a pan over medium heat, put the condensed milk, remaining brown sugar and butter, and the golden syrup. Cook everything together for 10 minutes, stirring occasionally, until the mixture has thickened and begun to turn a delicious golden brown. Remove the pan from the heat and stir the white chocolate through. Pour the mixture into the prepared baking tray and refrigerator overnight to set.

F. So, the big day has arrived and we're ready to assemble! Blend together the caramel coffee ice cubes and the remaining 2 cups of milk. Drizzle a generous amount of your thick caramel sauce around the inside of the glasses and then divide the blended coffee evenly between the glasses. Top with whipped cream and another drizzle of caramel sauce. Chop your caramel fudge into small ½-inch wide squares and sprinkle some onto the cream. Stick 2 pretzels into each glass, and balance 2 coffee beans in the cream too. Sprinkle on the caramel sprinkles, prepare your sweet tooth (you may wish to ring ahead to the dentist), and enjoy!

24. Biscotti Frappuccino

Serving Sizes: 2

Duration: 5 minutes

Ingredient List:

- 2 pieces of biscotti + crumbs
- 1 ½ cups milk
- 1 ½ cups vanilla ice cream
- 1 ½ cups fresh coffee

OOOOOOOOOOOOOOOOOOOOOOOOOOOOOOOOOOOOOOO

How to Cook:

A. Into a blender, add the coffee and milk and mix together.
B. Then, add the vanilla ice cream, biscotti, and 1 cup of ice. Blend until smooth.
C. Serve in 2 tall glasses, and sprinkle biscotti crumbs on top to garnish. If you don't have crumbs, pulse another biscotti in the blender to create some.

25. Churro Iced Coffee Float

Serving Sizes: 4

Duration: 20 minutes + overnight refrigeration

Ingredient List:

- 8 shots espresso
- 5 oz. sweetened condensed milk
- 4 cinnamon sticks
- 4 scoops vanilla ice cream
- 4 tsp. sugar
- 4 tsp. cinnamon
- 2 ½ cups cream soda
- 1 ½ cups milk
- 1 tsp. vanilla extract

OOOOOOOOOOOOOOOOOOOOOOOOOOOOOOOOOOOO

How to Cook:

A. In a pan over low heat, stir together the sweetened condensed milk, milk, and cinnamon sticks.

B. Cook the mixture down on low heat for about 8 minutes, giving the cinnamon plenty of time to infuse Stir so that the milk combines.

C. Remove from the heat and stir in the vanilla extract. Remove the cinnamon sticks.

D. Pour the cinnamon milk into a jar and refrigerate until you're ready to use it, or for at least 10 minutes until it's cooled down.

E. Mix the sugar and cinnamon together.

F. Divide the cinnamon milk mixture evenly between the 4 glasses, and then add 2 shots of espresso to each.

G. Add in a handful of ice, and then fill the glasses up to ¾ of the way full with cream soda.

H. Add a dollop of vanilla ice cream into each glass (and watch the magic happen!) and then sprinkle a little cinnamon sugar on top of each.

26. Maple & Almond Cold-Brew Coffee

Serving Sizes: 6-8

Duration: 35 minutes

Ingredient List:

- 1 cup coffee beans (or enough ground coffee as you would use to make 6-8 cups)
- 8 tbsp. maple syrup
- 3 ½ cups almond milk
- Pinch of salt

OOOOOOOOOOOOOOOOOOOOOOOOOOOOOOOOOOOO

How to Cook:

A. Prepare the cold brew by using whatever your preferred method, but using old water, and then place into the refrigerator overnight.

B. The next day, pour the maple syrup into a pan and heat it on low heat to just melt it. Add a good pinch of salt and stir well. Then, remove from the heat.

C. Strain your cold brew, to remove any grains, into a large pitcher, filled 1/3 of the way with ice cubes.

D. Stir in the almond milk and the maple syrup, once it has cooled a little, and enjoy!

27. Espresso & Tonic

Serving Sizes: 1

Duration: 5 minutes

Ingredient List:

- 3 ½ fl oz. tonic water
- 1 shot light-medium espresso (as a ristretto)
- ½ tsp. orange extract
- Dried or candied orange peel to garnish

ooooooooooooooooooooooooooooooooooooooo

How to Cook:

A. Add a few ice cubes into a tumble.
B. Pour the tonic water and orange extract into the tumbler, and give it a light stir.
C. Pour the espresso gently into the glass off of the back of a spoon, creating the cool effect where the coffee floats on top of the water.
D. Drop in your orange peel.

28. Cookie Dough Iced Coffee

Serving Sizes: 2

Duration: 20 minutes + at least 2 hours refrigeration

Ingredient List:

- 3 tbsp. white sugar
- 2 ½ tbsp. brown sugar
- 2 cups fresh coffee
- 2 scoops vanilla ice cream
- 2 tbsp. butter
- 1 cup milk
- 2/3 cup chocolate chips
- ½ cup plain flour
- ¼ tsp. vanilla extract

OOOOOOOOOOOOOOOOOOOOOOOOOOOOOOOOOOOO

How to Cook:

A. First, let's make cookie dough! Mix together the white sugar with the brown sugar, 1/3 of a cup of chocolate chips, and the butter until well-combined. Then, add the vanilla extract and 2 tbsp. of water. Finally, stir in the plain flour to create a dough. Then, shape it into a log and wrap it in greaseproof paper. Refrigerate for 2 hours.

B. 15 minutes before you want to make the coffee, take the vanilla ice cream out of the freezer to soften.

C. Cut the cookie dough into small chunks, and stir however many you like through the softened vanilla ice cream.

D. Into a blender, add the coffee and milk.

E. Then, add the vanilla cookie dough ice cream and the remaining 1/3 of a cup of chocolate chips. Blend until smooth!

F. Add a handful of ice to tall glasses and divide the cookie dough coffee evenly between them.

29. Spiced Mexican Iced Coffee

Serving Sizes: 4

Duration: 40 minutes + refrigeration time

Ingredient List:

- 6 cloves
- 4-star anise
- 4 cinnamon sticks
- 4 fl oz. coffee liqueur
- 4 tbsp. chocolate sauce
- 4 tbsp. heavy cream
- ¾ cup ground coffee
- ¼ cup white sugar
- ¼ cup brown sugar
- Cinnamon sprinkles

OOOOOOOOOOOOOOOOOOOOOOOOOOOOOOOOOOO

How to Cook:

A. Take a saucepan and pour 5 cups of water and add in the cinnamon sticks, cloves, and star anise.

B. Add the white and brown sugar and stir until they're dissolved, bringing the mixture to a

C. Then, lower the heat to a simmer and leave for 25-30 minutes for all of the flavors to infuse.

D. Remove from the heat, and add the ground coffee. Stir and then cover the pan, and allow the coffee to steep for 5 minutes.

E. Pour the coffee through a sieve or filter to remove the grounds and spices and then refrigerate until cool.

F. When you're ready to assemble your drink, put a tbsp. of chocolate sauce into the bottom of each glass. Then, add a handful of ice cubes and pour on the coffee liqueur.

G. Divide the refrigerated coffee between the glasses.

H. Pour 1 tbsp. of heavy cream over the top of each glass off of the back of a spoon, so that it sinks in gradually.

I. Sprinkle with cinnamon and enjoy!

30. Vanilla Iced Coffee

Serving Sizes: 14

Duration: 15 minutes

Ingredient List:

- 1 cup coffee
- 1 tsp. vanilla extract
- ½ cup milk

ooooooooooooooooooooooooooooooooooooooo

How to Cook:

A. Add 1 cup of water to a pan and add the sugar too. Bring the mixture to a boil and stir so that the sugar dissolves.
B. Then, add the vanilla extract and remove the pan from the heat to cool.
C. Add a handful of ice cubes to a glass, and pour in the milk.
D. Then, add the cup of coffee in over the top, and add vanilla syrup to taste. Usually, a tsp. and a half is a good amount, but the choice is yours!

Author's Note

T H A N K   Y O U

Not many people do this, but I grew up under difficult circumstances where nothing was handed to me, and the only way forward was with your best effort. At some point, people started recognizing me for my talent in the kitchen despite my young age, and I've only worked harder from there!

Because I am constantly trying to improve my work, I would really appreciate your help. Sure, I always ask my friends and family for their feedback on my newest projects but, whether they want to accept it or not, there's always some sort of bias because they don't want to hurt my feelings by criticizing my work. Thus, I need a neutral pair of eyes — that's where you come in!

If you're up for it, I would appreciate you telling me what you think of my cookbooks. Are the recipes easy to follow? Did you get stuck somewhere? Are the measurements laid out? Any suggestions you may have are welcome. After all, cookbooks are only helpful when you actually understand them! Incorporating your ideas and suggestions into my new projects will be my show of eternal gratitude because you can only be the best at something by constantly improving and being open to change.

Thanks!

Alicia T. White

About the Author

Alicia had a tough childhood and had to take care of her siblings early. Although they often helped her with making the beds and washing, Alicia was responsible for cooking since she was the oldest of six. Being in the kitchen was still very difficult at her age, but she learned her way around the stove and oven throughout the years.

Whereas her first dishes were practically inedible, burnt rice and mushy pasta… Eventually, she turned to the oven for help as many of the dishes she wanted to make were too complicated. Nonetheless, her baked casseroles were amazing! Most importantly, they were simple and required way less clean-up.

At first, they were simple pasta bakes, but once Alicia got the hang of things, she was baking all sorts of meals. When it came to spreading the word of her delicious cooking, having 5 siblings was extremely advantageous. Soon, neighbors were placing orders for some of her casseroles! Eventually, Alicia was doing so well with the business that she hired extra help. Now it's one of the most affordable yet popular weeknight casserole services in the mid-West!

Today, she still lives with her siblings and is working hard to teach them about the family business that led them out of poverty. She likes to publish cookbooks on casseroles and one-pot meals in her free time— basically anything quick and easy. Her motto is, "If a seven-year-old can't make it, it isn't simple enough!"